THE
BOOK
OF
ERRORS

ANNIE COGGAN

THE
BOOK
OF
ERRORS

WRITING BY MARK HAGE

INTRODUCTION BY BRIGID HUGHES
DESIGN BY NOËL CLARO

A PUBLIC SPACE BOOKS

A Public Space Books
PO Box B
New York, NY 10159

A Public Space gratefully acknowledges the generous support of the
Drue and H. J. Heinz II Charitable Trust, the Chisholm Foundation,
the New York State Council on the Arts, the Amazon Literary
Partnership, and the corporations, foundations, and individuals
whose contributions have helped to make this book possible.

Library of Congress Control Number: 2021930531
ISBN: 978-1-7345907-9-1
Distributed by Publishers Group West (PGW)

Design by Noël Claro

www.apublicspace.org

9 8 7 6 5 4 3 2 1

For my muses and protectors,
Caleb and Madeline

TABLE OF CONTENTS

IN HER RENDERINGS OF SPACE, ANNIE COGGAN reimagines history by altering architecture. She invites us to alternative conclusions to defined events, through improbably balanced chairs, textures of no existence in architectural fact, and dreamscapes of color that cannot be purchased at the outlet.

The Book of Errors is the tale of three architects who shaped and altered the stories of three iconic American spaces. It takes its title from the preservation missteps brought on by indelible preconceptions of those involved. In the General Henry Knox Museum, an architect reconstructs a house based on an inapplicable childhood memory. In Fraunces Tavern, the architect does diligent research but ignores that a building is also something lived in. In the Betsy Ross House, its architect believes the role of preservation is to superimpose myth on history.

In parallel text by Mark Hage, the portraits entwine the factual and the imagined, mirroring and expanding storytelling and form.

With Henry Knox, in 1919, Jane Watts, known as Miss Watts, persisted in wanting to reconstruct the original 1794 house, which had been de-molished for a railroad station. Her want and basis was a memory of a long-ago childhood visit to the house. At Fraunces Tavern, the architect William Mersereau was hired to restore the structure to its 1700s plan, despite two fires and expansions that had removed nearly every trace of its origins, and with barely any original recollections to rely upon. At the Betsy Ross House, the architect R. Brognard Okie's reputation gave him the status and license to renovate the building in the 1930s according to his own personal preferences. He was known to have demolished a recently constructed chimney of his own design and have had it replaced with corrections at his own expense.

In paper constructs that embellish scale and perspective, a house becomes a memorial to Miss Watts. In interior vignettes, another becomes an emblem of artifice. And a museum becomes a tribute to symbols of caste and class.

It is through these imagined architectures that *The Book of Errors* invites us to new possibilities, to histories that may or may not have happened, but that become possible stories of our mind, each in our unique way. —Brigid Hughes

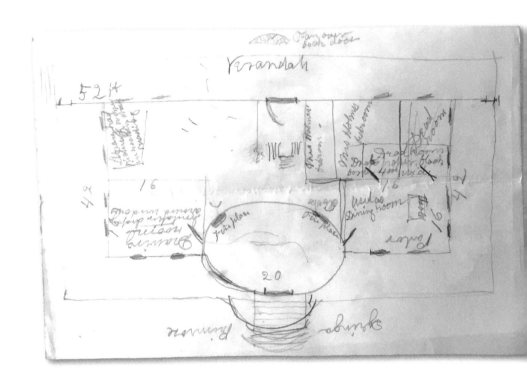

Drawings sent by Miss Watts to William E. Putnam, architect

RE-CONJECTURE
Miss Watts and Her Architect

General Henry Knox Museum

Miss Watts,
Daughters of the American Revolution,
(member number 23888)
to William E. Putnam:

"Dimensions of Montpelier."
"Recollections of Montpelier."
"Inside measure of the house: 32 ft. [...]
The large timbre used making it—55 ft front. 48 ft. deep."

WM. E. PUTNAM

ALLEN H. COX

PUTNAM & COX
ARCHITECTS
114 STATE STREET · BOSTON. MASS.
TELEPHONE · FORT HILL 560

BOSTON. MASS.. Oct. 15, 1919.

Miss Mary J. Watts,

Thomaston, Maine.

Dear Miss Watts:

It seems that the death of the architect, Henry W. Longfellow was "greatly exaggerated." It turns out that another Mr. Longfellow was the one unfortunate enough to lose his life.

We have been in communication with his office, but have not yet found him in. When we do, we will try to get hold of the drawings, before he can be overtaken by a similar fate.

We will let you know, when anything is accomplished.

With best regards from Mr. Cox and myself,

PUTNAM & COX
114 STATE STREET
BOSTON, MASS.

BOSTON, MASS.
OCT 15
3 PM
1919

Miss Mary J. Watts,

Thomaston, Maine.

William E. Putnam, Putnam & Cox Architects, State Street, Boston, MA, to Miss Watts:

"It seems that the death of the architect, Henry W. Longfellow was 'greatly exaggerated.'"

Dec. 10, 1920

Dear Miss Watts:

It is indeed a pleasant surprise to receive our check from Captain Tobey, and, we suspected, at once, that you had had a hand in steering him to action....

I really think, we can come pretty near to reproducing it now, with all the data we have collected, and, I should suppose that it would be well, as you say, to have the Architects plan showing what you propose to do....

Very truly yours,
William E. Putnam

Nov. 22, 1921

Dear Miss Watts:

The evidence, even of eye witnesses, as to the probable plans of the Knox House are so at variance that we have to consider it carefully and test each bit by things that we are sure of from a practical standpoint, and also from the photograph....

I wish you would read carefully Miss Miller's description and check it up with your remembrance. Also, if she is still living, I should think that a talk between you and her might clear up many of the points about which a difference of opinion seems to exist....

A very hard thing for us to accept is that the main rooms were only 16-0" square, and yet are spoken of as being very large, but, so many people agree upon this and the over all dimensions of the house, that we are compelled to believe that its impressiveness was due to the fact that all of those who remember it were small children at the time....

We shall look forward with great interest and curiosity to your next communication.

Yours very sincerely,
William E. Putnam

April 20, 1923

Dear Miss Watts:

Yours of the 19th arrived this morning, enclosing the three letters that Mrs. Holstein has written to Mrs. Wilson and to you. I have made memos from them so do not need them any longer.

My idea in suggesting that I would go to her house instead of troubling her to come in here, was entirely to save her trouble, and not to work out the plans with her as she seems to have assumed....

I judge from the tone of your letter that if in my opinion after seeing the plans the information is valuable, that you would not object if I bought it from her at an expense not exceeding $100.00.

Very truly yours,
William E. Putnam

May 17, 1924

Dear Miss Watts:

Your nice letter of May 15 arrived. We are glad that you had a successful trip home. It is too bad that you cannot find Mr. Gerry's plan....

We have had the smaller photograph enlarged and reproduced by perspective methods the plan, using the scale of the window glass which is given in a number of places and so is probably correct. We find that the plan from this picture corresponds exactly with the plan from the daguerreo-type and these strangely enough again correspond to the Gerry plan, a tracing of which you gave us.

This does not, however, make the rooms as small as the notes that you put on that plan....

Very truly yours,
William E. Putnam

PUTNAM & COX
ARCHITECTS
114 STATE STREET · BOSTON, MASS.
TELEPHONE · FORT HILL 560

BOSTON, MASS., June 2, 1922.

Miss Mary J. Watts,
Thomaston, Mass.

Dear Miss Watts:

I am very sorry you didn't have time to get into the office but I hope for better luck next time.

I am sending you another tracing of the plan that Professor Fowler drew from the one that his mother sketched from memory after twenty-five years. We sent you one of these on November 22, 1921 together with a copy of his letter and notes.

I am sorry not to have answered your letters more promptly but, I have expected every day that you would turn up at the office.

I wrote a letter to Mr. Strout sometime ago, and on April 6 got a letter from E. S. Copeland, whom he had asked if he could give any information. Mr. Copeland could not, but, he says that after the ground gets settled he thinks there can be found some traces of the old foundation. I would suggest, therefore, upon your arrival in Thomaston, you see if anything can be discovered of the old foundation, and we not go any further with the plans until you report. If nothing can be found, we can complete our drawings, and, I think, we will be near enough to the truth to satisfy everybody.

In regard to that sketch of Professor Fowler, it is rather interesting to see how completely his mother ignored doorways and fireplaces.

With best regards, I am

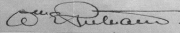

"I am sorry not to have answered your letters more promptly but, I have expected every day that you would turn up at the office."

"I think, we will be near enough to the truth
to satisfy everybody."

dimensions for the front of the house.

The proportions worked out are 76' x 40'. You see this does not make the house much larger than the proportions we arrived at the other day, but greater length and lesser depth improved the plan tremendously. We feel so sure that the photograph cannot lie and also so sure that an Architect with Bulfinch's work familiar to him would have designed a house about like this, that we hope you will be willing to have us work up the plans on these dimensions.

You were very kind to suggest paying $500.00 on account and while we had not intended to ask you for any money until the plans were completed, it would be very nice to have that money now.

With best regards.

WEP/C

Very truly yours,

PUTNAM & COX

PER *William E. Putnam.*

PUTNAM & COX
114 STATE STREET
BOSTON, MASS.

Miss Mary J. Watts,
Thomaston, Maine.

"While we had not intended to ask you for any money until the plans were completed, it would be very nice to have that money now."

WILLIAM E. PUTNAM

ALLEN H. COX

PUTNAM & COX
ARCHITECTS
114 STATE STREET
TELEPHONE, CONGRESS 0560

BOSTON   May 23, 1924.

Miss Mary J. Watts,
    Thomaston, Maine.

Dear Miss Watts:

Thank you very much indeed for your check of $500.00,
the receipt of which we enclose.

We cannot understand how the photographs could be so
wrong nor how Mr. Gerry when he drew a plan obviously to scale could
have been so far off in the dimensions of the rooms. If we make the
house as deep as 60', it is obviously impossible to keep the front
room only 16' or 17' deep and have a Library next to it that oc-
cupies the northwest corner without making that Library a great deal
longer than the main room, and the windows shown on the photograph
on the side being only four and very nearly regularly spaced, could
not very well hit on those rooms unless there were three in the
Library and only one in the large room, which it seems would be impossible.

Again, if the house is only 64' wide, it is impossible to
start the stairs some distance from the end wall of the hall and
get them up over a door going into the back hall.

We feel that it is too bad we haven't got Mrs. Holsten's
evidence, although of course, it may prove valueless. Mr. Cox is
going to see her and try to get some information out of her without
going to much if any expense. It may be that now knowing that we
have decided to go ahead without paying much attention to her plans,

"We cannot understand how the photographs could be so wrong."

THE "RESTORATION" of FRAUNCES' TAVERN

Sons of the Revolution Will Reopen Famous House Now Radically Changed—Architect Replies to Sharp Criticism of the Transformation.

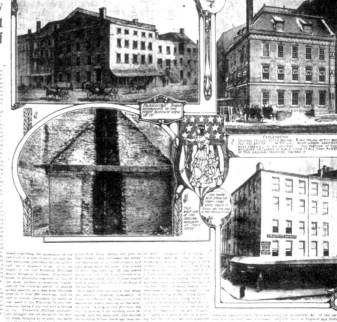

AMONG the historic landmarks to be found in New York none is more famous than Fraunces' Tavern, the old hostelry on the corner of Broad and Pearl Streets, in whose "Long Room" Washington bade farewell to his Generals at the close of the War of Independence, and where, during the colonial and Revolutionary days of the Republic, occasions speechmaking meetings and social functions were held. Since the time of Washington the tavern has been almost destroyed, on two occasions, by fire. Finally, about a year ago, it came into the hands of the Sons of the Revolution, who require that on May 1 it will be reopened as the headquarters of the society and as a public museum of historic antiquities. Preparatory to this reopening, the building has undergone a complete "restoration," as a result of which, according to statements made by the officers of the society, the tavern will once more appear exactly as it was when it was first built, more than two centuries ago. These statements, however, have not been met with entire acquiescence. [...]

How Fraunces's Tavern Was Restored

By William H. Mersereau

FRAUNCES Tavern was originally a private residence. It was erected on land conveyed by the Stephanus Van Cortlandt, one of the Dutch magnates, to his son-in-law, Etienne De Lancey about the year 1700. It was occupied for a time by Col. Joseph Robinson, and later by De Lancey, Robinson & Co. as a warehouse. The De Lancey of this town conveyed also his success in the French war, and later cemented as a loyalist Colonel of the Revolution. Their business was in European and East India goods and all sorts of army supplies, for which they were purveyors.

Turned into a Tavern.

Col. Robinson was living in the house in January, 1762, when we find it advertised for sale at the Merchants' Coffee House. The Colonel died in March of that year, but the partnership was not dissolved until December, 1762. Their counting house had already been passed by deed, on the 15th of January preceding, into the ownership of Sam Fraunces, who opened it as a tavern under the sign of "Queen Charlotte," or the "Queen's Head." There had been a tavern before with this sign, but the distant, for the Head, unless altered, was not the same.

It is appropriate here to give Fraunces's own description of his house as it was in 1776, an external appearance to which it has now been restored. [...]

When Spring Awakens in Manhattan

The Very First Signs Are to be Seen in Sheltered Back Yards — Then the Parks Begin to Awaken and the Birds Sing of the New Conditions—All Before the Open Country Shows the Change.

HE approach of Spring's approach and the first evidence of her presence can be seen by the town dweller more easily than by his country cousin. [...]

RE-IMAGINATION

Fraunces Tavern

"They then turned to the building itself.
 Here they were met with some encouragement."

—*William Howard Mersereau, architect*

"At 12 o'clock the officers repaired to Francis' Tavern, in Pearl Street, where Gen. Washington had appointed to meet them and to take his final leave of them.... After partaking of a slight refreshment, in almost breathless silence, the General filled his glass with wine."
—Memoirs of Colonel Benjamin Tallmadge (1858)

"In reply to the criticism that has been raised..."
—William Howard Mersereau, restoration architect of Fraunces Tavern (1907)

"With a heart full of love and gratitude I now take leave of you. I most devoutly wish that your latter days may be as prosperous and happy as your former ones have been glorious and honorable."
—General George Washington (1783)

Here are the Sons of the Revolution, those who owned the building, encouraged by Mr. Mersereau's restoration of Sunnyside, what more a precedent to engage an architect than him who restored Washington Irving's home. An architect born on Staten Island, residing alone in Bedford-Stuyvesant, with offices on lower Broadway.

His task, to restore the tavern, damaged by two fires and expansions, to its original condition. They did not know what that looked like. "With the exception of the slight description left by Fraunces himself, nothing of any moment was found."

Under candlelight, the dance master Henry Holt would host
balls and pantomimes at the tavern. (1738)

That meeting of the veterans of the Revolution would be
attended by Alexander Hamilton and Aaron Burr,
the week before their duel. In that space, there was
still hope no such incident would occur. (1804)

It does not matter within the room, but the new added roof
will not be a typical hip roof. Sloping sides surrounded by
a balustrade would be opted for.

"On passing the Washington statue... I thought I heard a loud
sobbing... I said: 'Why weepest thou?' He said:
'Hast been to Fraunces's Tavern lately and witnessed
the scoundrelly piece of vandalism that they have perpetrated
upon that hallowed building, with whose walls I embraced
my loved comrades?'"

—Letter to the *New York Times* (1906)

"If those who hold to the opinion that 'nothing of the old tavern is left
after this restoration' would really investigate matters... not a stick of
the old timber has been removed that could be possibly left."

—William Mersereau, architect (1907)

"How can men or women, who are pledged to preserve
evidences of our country's history, give their consent to such
destructive work?"

—Letter to the *New York Times* (1907)

"If it would only be presented honestly for what it really is."

—Ada Louise Huxtable (1965)

Birthplace of Old Glory, 1909
go past Berger dry goods, and it's just before the lamps

RE-CONFIGURATION

Betsy Ross House

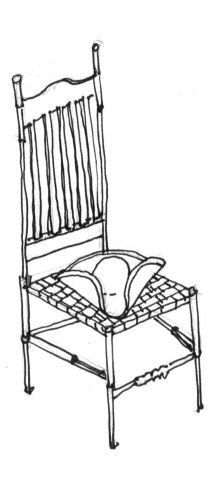

RICHARDSON BROGNARD OKIE,
COUNTRY-SQUIRE ARCHITECT, BORN 1875

ALMA MATER
University of Pennsylvania (est. 1740)

AFFILIATION
American Institute of Architects, Devon Horse Show

KNOWN FOR
Domestic stage sets, the choreography of domestic rituals (bedrooms
with canopies, Chippendale highboys)

NEMESIS
Archaeological data

STYLE
Colonial Revival; exaggerated gentility; a life of simplicity
and organization

MAJOR COMMISSIONS
Daughter's dollhouse (c. 1910), Pennsbury Manor, colonial estate of
Pennsylvania's founder (1936), Betsy Ross House (1937)

FAVORITE MYTH
Anything about the Titans

HOBBIES
Wood wall paneling, designing handmade historical hardware
(fasteners, joints), high-quality fakes

FOND OF
Yard sales

CAN'T ABIDE
Automobiles, modern appliances

ELIZABETH (BETSY) ROSS ASHBURN CLAYPOOLE (NÉE GRISCOM)

ARTISAN, BORN 1752

APPRENTICESHIP
John Webster, London-trained upholsterer of fashionable interiors

AFFILIATIONS
Society of Friends (resigned to marry John Ross), Free Quaker
meetinghouse (early member)

KNOWN FOR
repairing tents, stuffing mattresses, hand-sewn bedskirts,
draperies, flags; five-point stars

NEMESIS
six-point star

FAVORITE PASTIME
long evenings of tales

FAVORITE MYTH
Icarus. Wax would not do. Silk is what was needed.

FAVORITE POSSESSION
a small silver snuffbox marked with initials

UNCONFIRMED REPORT
General George Washington walking into her shop at
239 Arch Street to request a flag for the new republic

CONFIRMED REPORT
leading flag maker for the U.S. Arsenal on the eve of the War of 1812

DURATION OF CAREER
sixty years plus

FOND OF
tomatoes, dark snuff, a good joke

NICKNAME
Quicksnip

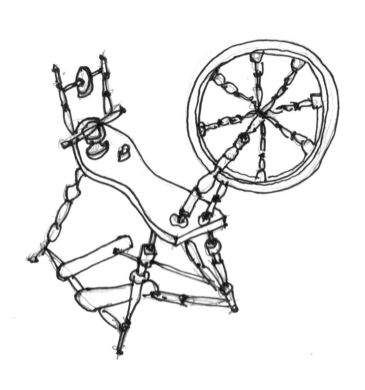

R. BROGNARD OKIE, ARCHITECT—RENOVATION PLAN
FIRST FLOOR—STREET LEVEL FOR THE SHOP

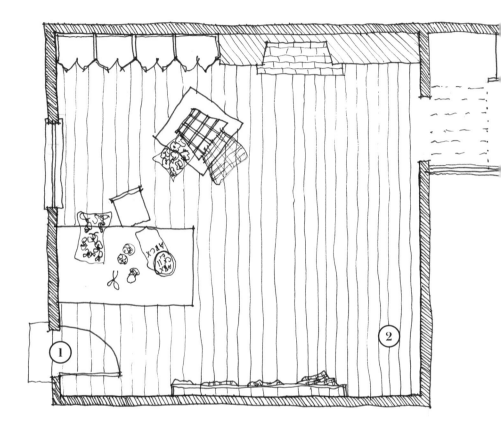

1. The entrance was moved to the opposite side of the street front, to create a more befitting entrance for General George Washington.
2. The renovation oriented the rooms toward the center staircase, to frame the dramatic domestic scenes.

3. R. Brognard Okie's attention to detail was legendary. The interior woodwork used his own hand-wrought nails.

4. The receiving room. Perhaps in this room General George Washington discussed the flag with Betsy Ross.

R. BROGNARD OKIE, ARCHITECT—RENOVATION PLAN
SECOND FLOOR

1. Daylight was a necessity for craftswomen like Betsy Ross. She chose to place her sewing materials away from the window.

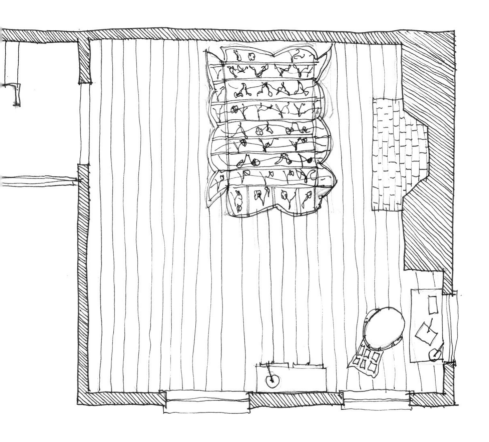

2. There was danger in supporting the American rebels. Tales are told of Betsy Ross sewing the first flag in these furthest reaches.

INDEX OF ANNIE COGGAN DRAWINGS

ACKNOWLEDGMENTS

David Gebhard, "The American Colonial Revival in the 1930s," Winterthur Portfolio (University of Chicago Press)

Michael Kammen, Mystic Cords of Memory: The Transformation of Tradition in American Culture (Vintage)

Patricia West, Domesticating History: The Political Origins of America's House Museums (Smithsonian Books)

GENERAL HENRY KNOX MUSEUM

Ellen S. Dyer, Montpelier: This Spot So Sacred to A Name So Great (The Friends of Montpelier)

Correspondence between Mary J. Watts and William E. Putnam, courtesy of the General Henry Knox Museum

FRAUNCES TAVERN

T. S. Affleck, letter to the editor, New York Times, September 12, 1906

Fraunces Tavern Museum, History and Archives Collections

Kent L. Harvick, Fraunces Tavern Block Historic District Designation Report (New York City Landmarks Preservation Commission)

Ada Louise Huxtable, reply to letter to the editor, New York Times, June 6, 1965

William H. Mersereau, "How Fraunces's Tavern Was Restored," New York Times, March 17, 1907

New York Preservation Archive Project

Benjamin Tallmadge, Memoir of Colonel Benjamin Tallmadge: Leader of the Culper Spy Ring (Kessinger)

BETSY ROSS HOUSE

Photograph of Betsy Ross house, courtesy of Library of Congress

James B. Garrison, Stone Houses: Traditional Homes of R. Brognard Okie (Rizzoli)

Mark Reinberger and Elizabeth McLean, "Pennsbury Manor: Reconstruction and Reality," Pennsylvania Magazine of History and Biography

Marla R. Miller, Betsy Ross and the Making of America (Henry Holt)